Mommy, What is Autism?

Written by Dr. Nikko Da Paz, BCBA
and Olabisi Thompson

Illustrated by Olabisi Thompson

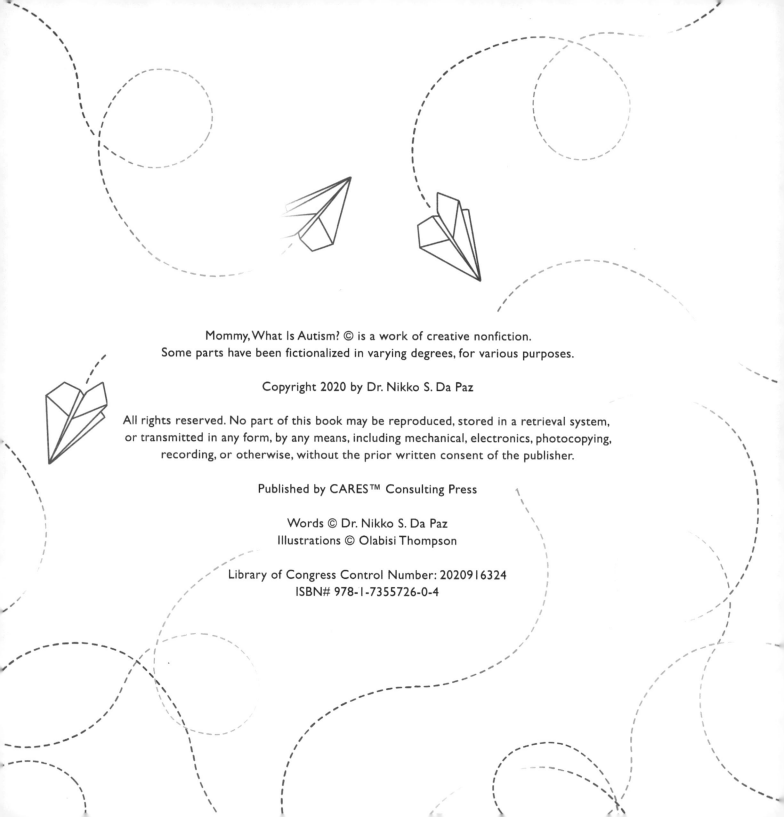

Published by CARES™ Consulting Press

Words © Dr. Nikko S. Da Paz
Illustrations © Olabisi Thompson

Library of Congress Control Number: 2020916324
ISBN# 978-1-7355726-0-4

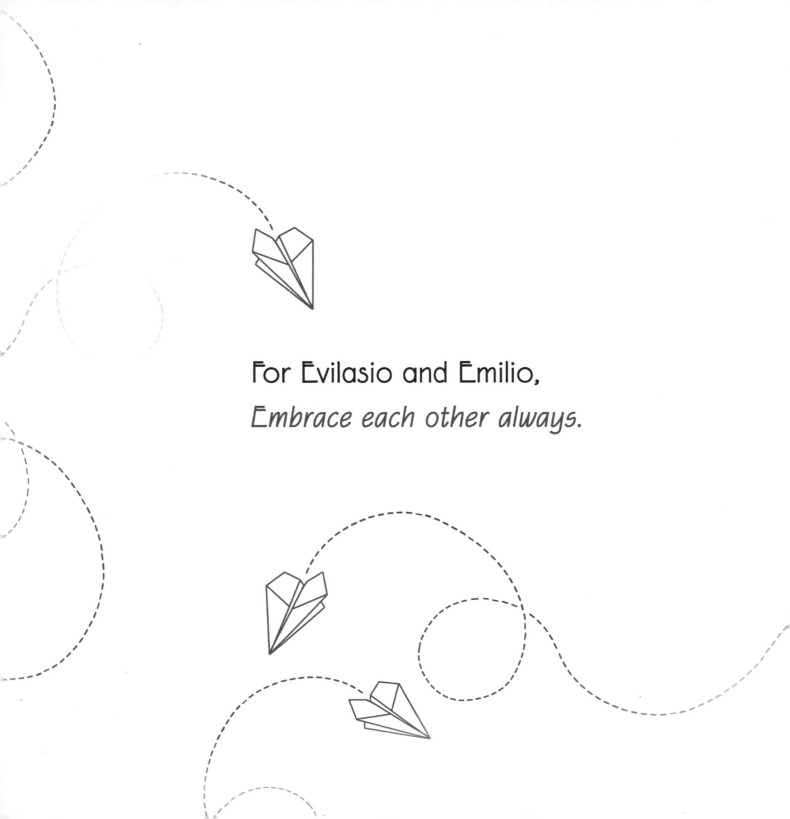

For Evilasio and Emilio,

Embrace each other always.

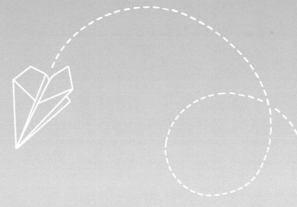

This is Papi and Meely.
They are **brothers**.

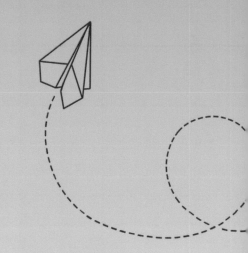

Meely
(little brother)

Papi
(big brother)

They are **alike** in many ways.

They are **different** too.

ONE DAY, they were **playing** a board game together.

Both brothers wanted to win.

Papi won the first round. "Yay!" Cheered Meely, throwing his hands in the air. Papi did not cheer. The next round, Meely concentrated really hard and won the game. "I won!" he said, dancing a victory jig.

Still, Papi did not cheer.

Meely was **confused**. "Hey, Papi, why didn't you say *good job* when I won the game?" **Papi did not respond.**

Instead, he stood up and went to **play** with something else.

ON ANOTHER DAY, the brothers were at the store with Mommy and Daddy...

Meely saw an awesome Rex-Ranger toy equipped with a green cape and light-up space boots!

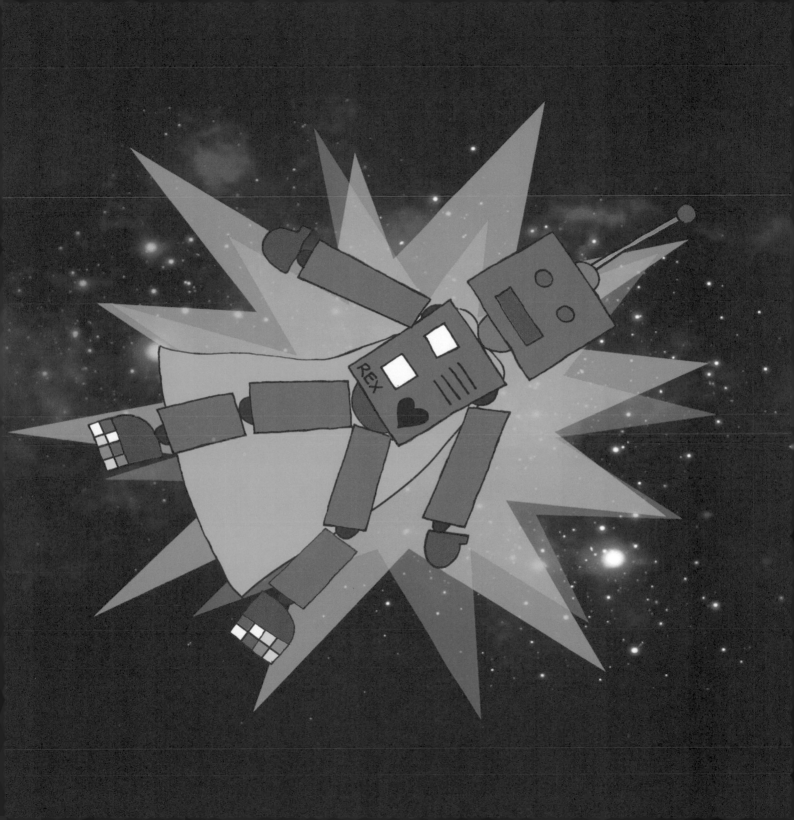

"Look Papi, this is the **coolest** toy ever!" said Meely.

Papi looked at the toy from the corner of his eye...

But he did not respond.

Meely was **confused**. "Hey, Papi, don't you think my toy is cool?" he asked his **brother**.

Papi **smiled** and picked up a different toy.

When they got to the check out line with Mommy and Daddy, the **brothers** put their toys in the basket.

"Boys, we are not buying toys today," said Daddy.

Meely was sad but he **listened**, and put his toy back on the shelf.

Papi did not do the same.

INSTEAD, PAPI SCREAMED AT THE TOP OF HIS LUNGS AND THREW HIMSELF ON THE GROUND, CRYING.

People were watching.

Mommy **crouched** on the ground with Papi and started to count.

"**ONE**, inhale...exhale.

Two, inhale...exhale.

Three, inhale...exhale.

Four, inhale...exhale.

Five, inhale...exhale."

Mommy continued to **count** and **breathe** with Papi until he was able to calm down.

Daddy **helped** Papi stand up, and held his hand. Mommy took Meely's hand, and the family walked to the car **together**.

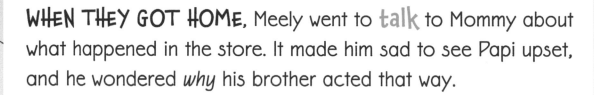

WHEN THEY GOT HOME, Meely went to talk to Mommy about what happened in the store. It made him sad to see Papi upset, and he wondered *why* his brother acted that way.

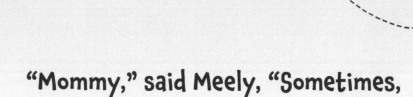

"Mommy," said Meely, "Sometimes, Papi does things that I don't like."

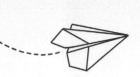

Mommy listened.

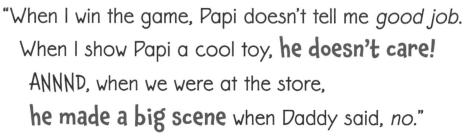

"When I win the game, Papi doesn't tell me *good job.*
When I show Papi a cool toy, **he doesn't care!**
ANNND, when we were at the store,
he made a big scene when Daddy said, *no.*"

"*I hear you,*" said Mommy, giving Meely a **big** hug.

"Thank you for telling me how you **feel**. You are wondering why Papi does some things different than you. *Let me explain...*

your brother has Autism."

Meely had heard that word before but he did not know what it meant.

He asked, "Mommy, what *is* Autism?"

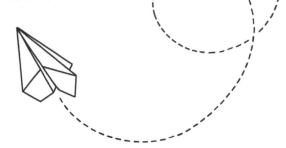

Mommy smiled, "Autism is a word used to describe **how your brother's BRAIN works.**

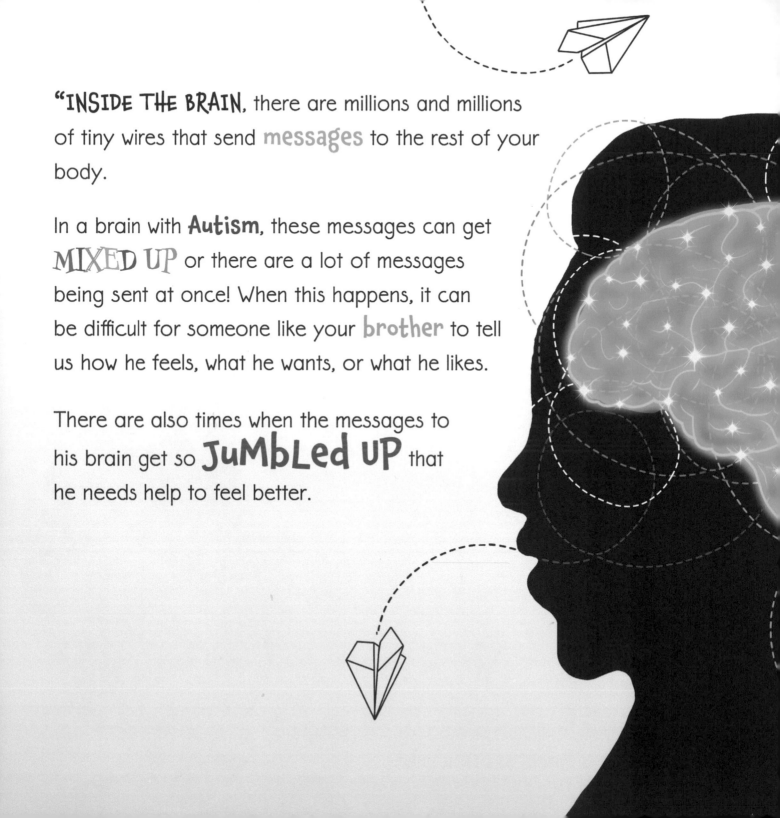

"INSIDE THE BRAIN, there are millions and millions of tiny wires that send messages to the rest of your body.

In a brain with **Autism**, these messages can get MIXED UP or there are a lot of messages being sent at once! When this happens, it can be difficult for someone like your brother to tell us how he feels, what he wants, or what he likes.

There are also times when the messages to his brain get so JuMbLed UP that he needs help to feel better.

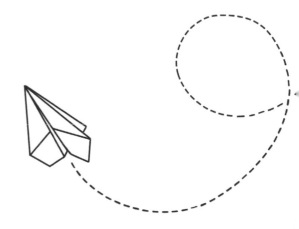

Meely **thought** about this very hard. "Is that why Papi has his own teacher at home?" he asked. "Yes," said Mommy, "Papi's teacher helps him to **communicate** how he *feels* as well as what he *wants* and *needs*. She shows Papi how to do lots of things. Mommy and Daddy help too." Meely's eyes got wide,

"I want to help too! How can I help?"

"You *are* helping!" Mommy said, smiling, "You help by **talking** to your brother, **playing** with him, and **aring** about him when he's sad or upset."

"AT THE SAME TIME, your brother's brain gives him the **ability** to do certain things really well, right?" Meely smiled. "That's true!

Mommy gave Meely another **big** hug
and a kiss on the forehead. "Thank you
for coming to talk to me," she said,
"I love you very much."

"I love you too, Mommy,"
said Meely, feeling better.

THE NEXT DAY, Daddy came home with a surprise for Papi and Meely.

One was wrapped in yellow paper with **trucks** on it. While the other surprise was wrapped in pink paper with **horses** on it.

What do you think was inside?

Both brothers were excited to open their presents.
The gift boxes revealed the **toys** they saw at the store!

"I like your **airplane**, Papi. The spinning propeller is really cool!" said Meely.

Papi did not speak.

Instead, he turned to his brother and handed him the shiny red toy. Meely **remembered** his talk with Mommy, and reached out to offer Papi the green Rex-Ranger.

Papi smiled a big smile. The **brothers** sat and played **together** enjoying each other's company.

Alike in many ways, and different too.

THE END

What Is Autism?

with

Dr. Nikko Da Paz, BCBA

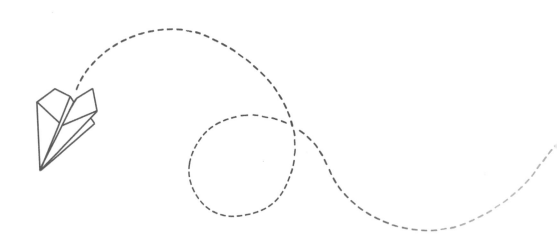

What Is Autism?
By Dr. Nikko Da Paz, BCBA

Explaining Autism to a child can be extremely difficult. That is the purpose of this book. A sibling, especially one close in age, might not understand why their brother or sister might act differently. They may even believe that their sibling receives special treatment. **Help them understand that Autism is a disorder of the brain**. It affects the way the brain works. In particular, it affects communication and social interactions.

Basic Components:

1. COMMUNICATION: **Their brother or sister might not talk or they may talk a little differently than other people**. When the sibling asks a question, tell them to silently count to 10 and wait for the individual with Autism to respond. **Use words, pictures, gestures, whatever it takes to connect and communicate. Above all, be patient.**

2. SOCIAL INTERACTION: **A person with Autism might experience difficulties interacting with others. They might want to interact but don't have the tools to do so correctly**. Help siblings interact by providing activities that they each enjoy (e.g. toys, baking, crafts, etc.). **Facilitate the play and guide them in turn taking. Encourage play interaction on a daily basis.**

3. REPETITIVE BEHAVIORS: **An individual with Autism may display repetitive behaviors such as rocking, bouncing on tippy toes, flapping arms, or saying things over and over**. A sibling might feel annoyed or embarrassed when their brother or sister with Autism starts to engage in repetitive behavior in public. Tell them it's important to focus on their brother or sister instead of others watching. Remind them that their sibling needs their love and compassion.

When overwhelmed with emotion, it is sometimes difficult for children with Autism to calm down. A simple method of counting and deep breathing can help to deescalate an intense moment and move your child closer to calm.

What to do:

1. **Get on your child's level.** If that means getting on the floor in the middle of a store, then do that. There have been many times that I found myself on the floor in department stores and at amusement parks. The most important thing is to concentrate on your child and not onlookers around you.

2. **Talk in a slow and calm tone.** Tell your child what you are going to do. Say: "Let's count together. One (take a deep breath in and blow it out). Two (take a deep breath in and blow it out)." First count to 10 and then ask if your child needs more. Say: "More?" If your child indicates they want more, then do it again. Keep checking in until they no longer want more.

3. **If possible, touch your child while completing this breathing technique.** This could be holding hands, hugging with arms, sitting with legs wrapped around the child, or whatever touching is comfortable for you and your child.

4. **Finally, be the calm you want to see.** It is important to calm yourself when attempting to calm your child. Your emotions and actions are a mirror to your child. Show them calm in the tone and volume of your voice, the slow pace of your movements, and your deliberate relaxed breathing.

Going to the Store

Going to the store with a child on the spectrum can sometimes become challenging, especially when they want something that they cannot have. Actually, going shopping with any child is challenging when they don't get what they want. Still, with children with Autism, it can get particularly difficult. It helps if you go out with a plan and give your child clear expectations and choices. Providing choices is key.

What to do:

Before leaving to go out, tell your child where you are going. It might be helpful to take a photo of the exact place and show that to your child before leaving.

GIVE YOUR CHILD A CHOICE of something they can have either in the store or after leaving the store.

IN STORE CHOICE: If there is a small toy or a favorite snack that you don't mind giving them, have it ready when they begin to display discomfort (e.g. crying, falling on the floor, etc.). Make sure you have items that your child really likes – I mean *really, really* likes. It needs to be something that is super motivating and your child sees it as the golden ticket. They will do just about anything to get it. Show them the two choices and ask, "Which one do you want?" Once they choose, help them to calm down first and then give it to them. Try using the breathing techniques to help with calming down. Having the item ready to give is extremely helpful.

BOTH – IN STORE AND AFTER STORE CHOICES: It is possible to use both techniques to make going to the store a pleasant experience. It doesn't hurt to have a bag (or box) of your child's favorites to use as choices while in the store and as incentives after leaving the store. Being prepared for the occasional public outburst makes it a lot easier to go out into the community with your child.

AFTER STORE CHOICE: Give your child two choices for something they can have after leaving the store. Using the same method mentioned above, show them the highly preferred choices and let them choose. If they begin showing discomfort while in the store, simply remind them of their choice: "First store, then _____." Have the item ready to give them once you leave the store.

Interventions for Autism

Applied Behavior Analysis (ABA) is an evidence-based intervention frequently used in the treatment of symptoms associated with Autism. Many children with Autism receive in-home support from ABA service providers. This means that a Behavior Technician (BT; also known as a Behavior Therapist and/or a Tutor) comes to the home Monday through Friday for three to five hours per day. As a parent of a child with Autism, our family had a BT coming to our house daily for more than ten years. Prior to becoming a Board Certified Behavior Analyst (BCBA) and starting my own ABA private practice, I was the BT going to the home and teaching children on the spectrum.

Our company, CARES™ Consulting, offers support for the entire family. We understand that Autism does not only affect the child, but the entire family unit. Oftentimes, some siblings might think their brother or sister with Autism has a daily play date because they see someone coming into their home every day bringing toys and activities. It is important to be mindful of brother or sister's feelings and provide activities for them as well.

What to do:

1. **Provide opportunities for your children to play games together.** Choose simple activities and encourage your children to take turns. It can be something as simple as throwing a ball or blowing bubbles.

2. Establish a time to do something with the sibling so that they receive special attention. For example, while their brother with Autism has session, read a book with them, make cookies, or just do something that they like to do. This way, each time the BT arrives, the brother/sister knows that he/she will get to do something fun as well!

3. Ask your Autism Service Provider if the sibling can be included in a game. At CARES™ we are mindful of siblings and include interactive play as a targeted goal. This encourages sibling interaction with a trained professional.

CPSIA information can be obtained
at www.ICGtesting.com
Printed in the USA
BVHW020834151121
621193BV00014B/434